Golfing

for the Emotionally Impaired

Written by: William Kennish

Illustrated by: Lisa Joey

Published by

Walrus Productions

Seattle

Published by **Walrus Productions**
4805 NE 106th St. Seattle, WA 98125

(206) 364-4365 fax (206) 362-2834

e-mail walrus@aa.net   Web Site: www.walrusproductions.com

Written by William Kennish
Illustrated by Lisa Joey
Layout and Typography by The Durland Group

Printed by Vaughan Printing, Nashville, Tennessee

Library of Congress Catalog Card Number 98-61344

Kennish, William (William Joseph), 1949-
        Golfing for the Emotionally Impaired / written by
        William Kennish; illustrated by Lisa Joey. -- 1st ed.
        ISBN 1-892851-18-0

        1. Golfing -- Humor. I. Title
        GV967.K46 1998   796.352'02'07
                                    QB198-1166

Printed in the United States of America

10 9 8 7 6 5 4 3 2 1

Dedication

To my wife, Renee, who let me spend the time to write this book, not that I couldn't have anyway if I really wanted to! (See my next book on Marriage)

To my son, Bill, who laughs at anything.

To all those golfers out there who were natural sources of material for this groundbreaking book.

And a particular thanks to Lisa- my illustrator, my niece and a great artist. Lisa would like to thank Denny for his patience in describing and demonstrating the basics of golf.

Introduction

Golf has evolved into a marvelous blend of physical prowess, mental acuity and technological achievement. All three of these have been discussed, debated and belabored in book after book in a desperate attempt to help all golfers shoot par (it just isn't going to happen folks!). But most people's success at enjoying golf depends as much on a fourth factor as the first three: their emotional control.

The inspiration for this book came one day when my wife and I were playing a beautiful course on Hilton Head Island on Christmas Eve.

We stood patiently on the tee watching the group ahead of us hit their second shots.

It was a gorgeous day and we were basking in the warm sun, just happy to be there and not in cold Philadelphia. One of the gentlemen had found the long grass around a hazard and hit a worm killer out.

Frustrated, he dropped another ball and proceeded to hit it about the same distance as the first.

Now clearly upset, he dropped a third ball and hit another shot, which was surpassed only by the first two. He reared back to throw his club but then, thinking better of it, turned and snapped the club in two across his knee.

I decided soon thereafter that someone needed to help these poor souls (or at least exploit their pathetic condition). As you will see, what resulted from that memorable day was an in-depth analysis of the game of golf from a slightly different perspective. Actually, the in-depth part is stretching it a bit, but facts are generally overrated anyway. It is, however, definitely a different perspective.

Since writing the book, I have heard more and more people confirming my belief that most golfers take the game way too seriously. Follow my simple suggestions and you should (this is a non-definitive warranty for you litigious players) find inner peace and pastoral bliss in your future golf games. Your score might suck, but you'll be smiling the whole time.

NICE DAY AT
THE CLUB DEAR?

By the way, most of my comments are framed as if I'm talking only about men. This is not that I'm a stereotypical male chauvinist pig, but it appears that men stress out much more at golf than women. I assume this is the result of a higher male intellect, but it could also be that women actually like to get out and enjoy the game. At one point in the past, I thought this might be the answer to the tension problem for us guys, so I bravely tried the female approach. Unfortunately, the course manager threw me off the course for wearing one of those frilly dresses.

As you read the book, you might get frustrated that you can't immediately master some of the techniques.

This is to be expected.

It's taken me 37 years of golfing to evolve to this higher level being with self control and low blood pressure. Unfortunately, my game didn't evolve as much, but that's what we're here about, isn't it? Just keep this book close at hand and perhaps a spare copy in the master bathroom. Keep reading it over and over until you at least stop kicking the dog and strangling the kids after those particularly bad rounds. But so much for the introduction, which no one ever reads anyway. Let's push on to the profound insights and psychological probing. I'll start out with the really big ideas. Even if you are skeptical, you should at least read the first chapter.

The mind you save could be your own.

Chapter 1. Scoring (in golf)

I didn't bother doing any research for this book, but I'm pretty sure this must be how golf began.

One day a couple of guys took up some sticks and went out to the fields on a nice day just to enjoy the moment. Seeing a couple of rocks in the field they tried to see who could hit the rock the farthest. After a while they wanted to add a little challenge (actually the guy who couldn't hit it very far made the sugges-tion; the one who hit it the farthest later invented baseball, but that's another story), ... so they started trying to see who could come closest to hitting a tree in the field.

The men enjoyed the game and over the months other friends joined in. Everyone had a good time trying to hit the tree and one clever fellow even suggested they try hitting a second tree, although it was met with reluctance by some of the more established "tree-bangers" (I guess it's obvious why that name didn't stick for the sport). Ironically, the rocks would often go down gopher holes and the treebangers considered this a great annoyance.

After about a year or two of this pastoral bliss, the Devil (Satan himself) became peeved at the contentment and joy being experienced by all of these middle-aged gentlemen (for some reason, even from day one, the sport was most appealing to middle aged men) and decided to sow some seeds of discontent.

TREE BANGING....the roots of golf.

He sent an agent to the group and after establishing himself as an accomplished treebanger, the agent suggested that it might be fun to keep score.

Over the next two years there evolved a form of match play where the players would go from tree to tree in groups of two, keeping track of the number of trees won. One of the unfortunate fallouts of this early period was the killing of most of the trees in Scotland, hence the wide-open rolling hills. In fact, twenty-three years later players were forced to carry their own small saplings with them and stick them in gopher holes so they would have something to shoot at.

Ah hah! Now you're really starting to see the history of the game.

Well, the players still weren't getting agitated enough for the Devil so he decided to see what else he could do to heighten the anxiety of the game. He noted that when people lost their balls (or rocks in those early days) they didn't worry too much about it since it only meant one tree and they played from dawn to dusk, sometimes getting in 150 trees by the end of the day.

He came upon a diabolic plan, one that would definitely cause tension and anxiety in all unsuspecting fools who decided to play the game. He had his agent point out to the more consistent players that even though they were more consistent, they often lost to players who would do horribly on a few trees but do well on the other trees.

These were the risk takers, and he convinced the consistent players to propose a revision to the game that would put them at a great advantage over these risk takers.

He suggested that there be a limited number of trees played and that the score accumulate. This way the risk taker would be properly punished for losing rocks and getting huge scores on individual trees.

The consistent players liked the idea and soon the game changed to cumulative score keeping.

The number of trees was initially limited to 47 but later changed to 18 for obvious reasons.

More Rules!

There were a couple of other scoring rules that evolved around this time and are probably worth mentioning.

To try to make the game a little more challenging, the players soon devised a reward and punishment scoring system for their match play.

They decided that if you could hit a tree, with a bird in it, carefully enough so that the bird didn't fly, you would get a point off your score for that hole.

If you were fortunate enough to hit a tree with an eagle in it (a very rare event) and the eagle did not fly, you got two points off.

Who knows where "par" came from and it's beneath me to just make something up.

And so goes the development of the par, birdie and eagle scoring system… I'm pretty sure. Some of you probably always wondered what in the world a birdie and eagle had to do with golf.

There were penalties defined at this time as well, and they had a lot to do with the farmer who owned the land where golf began.

THE EARLY DAYS of GOLF ON MR. BOGEY'S FARM
"Darn, another double MR. BOGEY!!"

His name was George Bogey, and if you hit one of his cows, you got a stroke added to your score for that tree.

If you were unlucky enough to hit more than one animal with a single shot, then you would get the appropriate number of strokes added.

Hence the terms bogey, double bogey, triple bogey and so forth.

Losing rocks, especially down gopher holes, obviously had to result in a penalty as well, so they added a couple of strokes for that.

That particular penalty never seemed very interesting so people just referred to it as a lost rock (and later a lost ball). There also exists a long list of other penalties that evolved over the years.

In Mr. Bogey's north 40, where some of the more accomplished players would go, there were relatively few trees.

This resulted in very long holes. Along a couple of those holes were ponds filled with many lily pads. On occasion, a player's rock would land on a pad and actually stay on top in plain sight. The early golfers were somewhat strong-willed and would wade out into the pond to take their next shot.

Unfortunately this resulted in the loss of a couple of the players and many contracted warts from the frogs in the pond.

To help prevent further losses, the players joined together and decided that these ponds were hazardous to their health and should be so labeled and avoided.

Joe Bumbly, not one of the more clever players, suggested that they call these ponds "Boo Boos", but thankfully Peter Clubber, a bright, young, up and coming treebanger, suggested that they simply refer to them as hazards.

This seemed popular with the other players and so the label stuck.

In honor of his stroke of genius, the players started referring to their sticks as clubbers, which was shortened to clubs later for the benefit of Mr. Bumbly who couldn't remember the full name.

As an aside, you'll be glad to know that Mr. Bumbly was eventually honored as well.

After he became head bartender of the group, he referred to his drinks as Boo Boos. The other players finally gave in and started referring to the drinks as Boos so that his feelings would not be hurt.

And so goes the evolution of the scoring system of golf, as well as some important historical tidbits on the development of the game.

The Devil's intent was fulfilled magnificently.

With so few holes to play and every stroke counting against you, the pressure mounted and anxiety ran very high.

To this day the Devil continues to monitor each player's game to make sure that just enough good shots are mixed in with the bad shots so that you all continue to play despite the swearing and sobbing after errant shots.

It was necessary for you to know all of this so that you will understand the importance of my very first tip:

DON'T KEEP SCORE
(the usual way)

FOR A GOOD TIME, TOSS THE SCORE CARD.

If you are playing against someone (for fun I hope) and feel you must keep score, be sure to play match play. Also be sure to make it a never-ending match, sort of like the golf tournaments now.

Notice how calm the pros are, putting six feet for $500,000. That's because they have made the tour a constant string of tournaments that never end; and they just keep accumulating money. You, of course, will accumulate matchbooks, but it amounts to the same thing.

If you are not playing against someone, set a mark like par or bogey or double bogey and see how many times you can reach your goal or even surpass it.

Don't worry about how bad your score is on one hole; there's always the next one.

You see a tournament on TV once in a while that uses a similar format, except they tend to set loftier goals and actually penalize you for bad scores. This must be to make the players suffer more, which everyone enjoys when watching television.

In fact, the only TV players that seem to be really having a good time are the Senior skins participants. Even in those games it seems to get a little less rowdy when they start playing for holes worth a few hundred thousand dollars. I know I tend to pay attention more to my game when I'm playing for that kind of money!

Putting for a 7!!

..This tip does create minor problems when it comes to club tournaments and handicapping, but these specialized subjects are dealt with in later chapters.

Now that we know how to keep score (or NOT) in our quest for inner peace . . .

Let us move on to our next subject . . . Equipment.

***

Chapter 2. Equipment

Remember, we're not discussing how to golf better but rather how to survive the emotional trauma of golfing. With this in mind, let's take a look at how there came to be 7,832 brands of golf clubs, 2,865 different golf balls and approximately 253,968 gadgets related to golf.

In the beginning, a stick and a stone sufficed as an excuse to get out and enjoy the weather.

As competition increased, the more clever players invented (or found) new stick shapes and different rock sizes.

"I...I've g..got to g..g..get one of th...those
n..new l...lo.long d..distance ro..rocks..."

A turning point was some years later when a tradesman decided to whittle a stick for a friend who was a
passionate player of the game.

He was clever in his design and produced a "club"
that looked something like a hockey stick.

His friend was soon winning tree after tree and
became the envy of the glen.

Other players asked the tradesman to whittle them a
stick and soon he was producing clubs for most of the
better players. (His name was Henry Graphite and
only recently has he been honored by having shafts
named after him.)

As with any successful business, Henry expanded his line of goods.

Unfortunately, his whittled wooden golf bags and shoes were not well received and he soon gave up the business.

Other tradesman took up where Henry left off, however, and within a few years there was a burgeoning industry related to the sport.

River dwellers from far away started exporting smooth and perfectly sized river stones for the treebangers to use and the clubs got fancier and fancier.

THE BEGINNING OF THE GOLF INDUSTRY

We don't have enough time to discuss in excruciating detail the development of all of the basic tools of golf.

I will just mention a few ... since you must be just dying to know.

First the glove. I think it's nice that they tried to keep the cost down by only selling one glove. But have you ever wondered why the left glove (for us normal right handers) and not the right? That's so you can fish around with your right hand in your pocket for a ball marker.

Pretty interesting, huh?

The dimples on the modern day golf ball were the result of a cruel joke.

Apparently a non-golfer bet his friend that golfers were so stupid that they would believe anything, so he took the nice smooth ball then in use and put dimples all over it, making up a story about how it would improve the aerodynamics.

Well, not only did they believe him but the design became the rage and to this day we continue to use balls with dimples.

The development of the tee came from a frenetic whittler trying to whittle a three foot high tea bag holder.

"But the guy told me the dimples would help the ball go straight!"

When asked what the little one inch stick was for that he was left holding, he replied with some frustration "Tea". The fellow, who happened to be an accomplished treebanger, grabbed it up and said "Good idea. My rock will sit on this perfect." ... And off he went to make history. (The early treebangers also used the tee to pick their teeth but that ended when the naked lady tees were invented.)

The golf cart was also invented at this time, although only the nobility were well off enough to use them.

Nobility being who they are, they insisted that they not sit directly behind the butt of the horse (did you think they were electric carts?).

So the creators of the golf cart were forced to figure out a way to put the cart before the horse, which of course stayed with us to this day as an expression describing something stupid.

Now let's talk about how golfers trying to be at one with the universe should equip themselves to make the outing a pleasant one.

Extensive research (by someone else) has shown that despite what the average golfer claims after every round, the clubs are not the problem for 98.13% of us. This suggests an interesting approach to maintaining tranquillity.

DON'T GET THE MOST ADVANCED CLUBS!

Always play with someone who has better clubs than you and don't be afraid to point out your disadvantage to your opponent on numerous occasions during the round. When you hit a bad shot be sure to tap your club on the ground and mumble.

This is understood by all golfers as "Darn club. New clubs would never have sliced that ball 72 yards into the woods." It's important that you also believe this so that you don't blame yourself.

But if you aren't supposed to blame yourself, who can you blame? That's why golf is such a frustrating if not perverse game.

You're standing still, holding a big club with a big head on it, trying to hit a ball that is just sitting there waiting to be hit. It isn't moving around trying to dodge you. When it doesn't go where you aimed, who's at fault?

Certainly not the ball. It was just sitting there.

So if you don't want to blame it on yourself and lose your composure, the clubs must take the fall.

That's why you shouldn't play with great clubs.

A caveat to this blame problem is the use of caddys, which introduces another entity that can be blamed as needed.

Unfortunately, it's difficult to convince anyone, even yourself, that the reason you hit the ball out of bounds is that the caddy didn't tell you not to.

However, there are occasionally excellent opportunities to lay the blame on the caddy, such as a shot to the green that falls short into the water.

You can confidently blame the caddy for giving you the wrong club (be sure to always use the club they suggest in case of this very event) or not telling you about the 30 mph headwind.

THE ART OF BLAMING YOUR CADDY

"Why didn't you tell me about the wind?"

As this book becomes the Bible of Golf, it might become more difficult to have clubs inferior to those of your opponent, as they will have undoubtedly read this book as well and will also be trying to use inferior clubs.

Keep at least two and preferably three sets of varying quality clubs in your garage. Until you know your opponent, go with the worst and work your way up.

A more subtle point for tall people is to never get long clubs. This simple tip can mitigate huge amounts of frustration. Note that everyone will tell you that you can't possibly be expected to hit the ball well with short clubs.

In reality, have you ever seen a 7 foot tournament player? That's because as soon as a tall guy starts playing the game, the short guys convince him to get extra long clubs.

This, of course, only makes it harder to hit straight since you're farther from the ball and you have more opportunity for error.

Quick tip
Beware of advice from friends!

"Are you SURE these extra-long, over-extended hyper-sized clubs will help my game?"

For those of you who have custom-made, oversized, platinum-coated, aerodynamically-designed clubs (with fancy head covers for even your irons!!!), keep in mind what your opponents are going to be thinking when you're straddling a stump and aiming through a maze of pine trees -- NICE CLUBS, HOTSHOT.

Now that's pressure!

The putter is by far the most important club in your bag, accounting for about half of your shots if you shoot par. (It accounts for about 2/3 of my shots but I don't count them all as full strokes.) It is also the source for immeasurable tension and frustration. It makes no sense at all not to be able to roll a little ball four feet into a hole that is amply sized. But in fact it happens all the time and you better be prepared or boom -- there goes your composure.

In the case of putting, style is more important than buying the right club.

Since everyone knows this, using old, gnarly clubs doesn't buy you any sympathy. What does work, however, are some subtle moves both before and after the putt.

Be sure to always stand behind your ball and dangle the club toward the hole.

This not only looks very professional but when combined with a quick recheck and nod after the bad putt, everyone knows that there must have been a misread because of the club dangle and not because you just whacked it three feet to the left.

You should also walk to the hole and tap down some spike marks. (Don't do this in a tournament. Someone brighter than me decided that spike marks are God's creation and one shouldn't fix them before putting.)

This clearly indicates that the green is in disrepair and you are not liable for where this one is going.

As a final move, if you miss by just a little, look at the putter face and give it a quick wipe.

The knowledgeable opponent will then know that you would have gone right in the hole but the club had a grain of sand on it that made it go left.

Ball selection is not that big of a deal, unless you're a guy and you choose those pink balls.

Cute as they are, this is a big mistake. If you hit many of those little dribblers with pink balls, you will eventually get the question: "Does your husband play?" This can increase the pressure of the match considerably.

If you are a woman, get the lower compression balls.

This is not because they will help you but because they will keep you from outdriving the men, which is why a guy invented the low compression ball in the first place.

"I gave Ethel those ultra-low compression
balls for her birthday...."

Here's another tip: Don't ever buy tees.

There are only five people in the country who actually buy tees and they are very wealthy. Everyone else goes around and picks up the lost tees from prior players or they get a handful of freebies in the clubhouse at the better clubs.

The exception to this rule is the naked lady tee, which is very hard to find. If you feel strongly about teeing your ball up on a naked lady, then you just might need to spring for a dozen.

I choose to hit my tee shots without a tee.

That way if I hit a good shot my opponent is very intimidated. If I hit a bad shot, not using a tee was clearly the reason.

So much for the basics.

As you can see, proper club set selection can make all the difference in your attitude.

But what about all those other gadgets available to golfers today? Will it help your game if you can use a little viewer to determine that it is 189 yards to the hole and not about 185 yards? Keep in mind that you've probably never hit the green from that far away and if you did, it was because you bladed it and it rolled for the last 50 yards.

Looks like it's 187 yards,
2 feet, 3 inches.

How about using strings of beads to keep score with? Since you shouldn't be keeping score in the first place (see Chapter 1), these beads could be used as prayer beads both before and immediately after hitting the ball. (It's beyond the scope of this book to address in detail the role of religion in golf.)

There are many ways to get you and your clubs around the course. Here again, the golf industry has developed many sophisticated gadgets to drag your clubs, prop up your clubs or you can simply jump into a cart and drive. The carts will range from those with no tops, dying batteries and flat tires (with a few empty cans passed along) to the luxury models installed with range-finders and pace beacons.

If you can afford a cart, get one.

Not that it will help your game, and it certainly won't help you lose weight, but it will be great to sit in a cart and relax while you wait for the three foursomes ahead of you to get off each tee.

ANOTHER TIP

Always look at delays as an opportunity for a nap rather than as a delay in your busy schedule.

This will keep the frustration down and, if played right with a few carefree comments, will drive your opponent to the brink of hysteria.

Develop patience if playing public courses.

Shoes are important since no person can be stress-free if their puppies are hurting. The tassels, however, should be carefully considered.

I believe they were added by the same fellow who added the dimples to the golf ball, or perhaps by his sadistic wife.

If you are comfortable with your manhood (this is for men only), then get the pretty tassels.

Unfortunately, I was not able to get any information on why shoe designers spend millions of dollars trying to make golf shoes waterproof and then put holes all over the shoes, but apparently they're a must if you are to look fashionable.

Speaking of fashion, clothing in golf is critical in maintaining your composure. Some people make fun of the plaid designs and short pants that are part of the history of the game, but they are important to your tranquillity. Wearing these clothes can create major distractions for your opponents. (Have you ever tried hitting a golf ball while you're giggling?) They will also prepare you for any unsightly garb your opponent might try to wear to distract you. So the bottom line is to wear the gaudiest outfit your spouse will let you keep in the house.

For the most part, the other zillion golf gadgets have little or nothing to do with hitting the ball. However, they do keep a lot of people employed and therefore I fully support their purchase.

Something for everybody.... everything for somebody.

It might also be noted that the right gadget can act as an excellent distraction from becoming frustrated.

For example, if you buy one of those soapy brushes for cleaning your irons and use it after every shot, you start looking forward to making your club nice and shiny rather than dwelling on the fact that you just shanked the ball into the water.

Think of those gadgets as little perks. In summary, equipment can be used to absorb the blame for just about every bad shot thinkable. If it isn't clear how, don't become impatient. Like anything else, it takes time to develop a complete repertoire of excuses.

***

Chapter 3. Rules and Etiquette

Earlier I described a number of rules in passing, none of which should be taken very seriously if you're not in a tournament. It doesn't hurt, however, to review some of the basic rules and their significance.

One of the biggy rules is that you are supposed to hit your own ball.

This seems obvious until you are both looking for lost balls in the rough. Why shouldn't it be first find, first swing? Try to carry lots of balls loose in the cart with different brands and numbers, so that you can always claim any ball found.

If your opponent presses you into declaring what ball you are hitting before starting, look for a new opponent. This guy is way too serious about the game.

Another rule is that you can't move your ball around in the fairway. From an emotional standpoint, this is not a good rule. Therefore, whenever you are playing for fun, feel free to adjust the lie so that your ball is not in a hole or in a clump of obnoxious weeds.

This is called winter rules but it sounds like a good idea for any season. Remember, at any time of the year, it's winter somewhere! (Teeing the ball up in the fairway is probably going too far, but with careful investigation you can probably find a little mound of grass that basically accomplishes the same thing.)

Improving your lie simply maintains the purity of the game.

There are a whole string of rules about penalty strokes but we all now know where those came from (see Chapter 1) so don't take them too seriously. Since you're not supposed to be keeping score anyway, what is important is to see how you would have done if you hadn't hit the ball into the bushes or the lake. So take a drop and keep going. But here is a subtle tip. Be sure to finish your search for your ball at the best possible position. If you're going to take a drop, it might as well be a good one.

If you make a par or birdie on one of these holes where you have taken relief from the hazard, you might put a little asterisk next to the score so your opponent thinks you are keeping track of the penalty strokes.

THE ART of REPLACING LOST BALLS
"I'll just drop one here."

If you read the rules of golf (not recommended), you will notice a lot of fuss about water hazards and penalty strokes for dropping out of these hazards. If you read further, however, you will notice that for "casual water" there is no penalty for dropping out of the water. Since I have never seen anything but water in a casual state, I consider all bodies of water to be casual. This relieves the pressure of feeling like you should be taking a penalty stroke.

I recently became curious about what makes a golf ball legal. Those ads that say the "ball is so lively they've been outlawed" intrigue me.

I went to my rules book and there I found my answer.

First it has to be under a certain weight and over a certain diameter. No big surprise there.

But then they talk about "Spherical Symmetry".

They describe testing 40 balls in 20 pairs and launching each ball around a different axis. Then they define the difference in carry and the time of flight and the statistical level of significance required.

By the time I finished wading through the rules my head was throbbing but I was still committed to golfing within the rules so off I went to my local golf shop. I was fortunate enough to find 12 golf shops within a two mile radius so I picked the one with the most meaningful name- "Montana Fred".

The people in the golf shop got real upset when I started launching golf balls about different axis. Turns out the manufacturer worries about all that stuff for us golfers. But now you know just how careful you have to be when deciding which ball to use.

There's even a rule about how you hit the ball. According to the rule, you must fairly strike at the ball with the head of the club. And you shouldn't push, scrape or spoon the ball.

Finally a rule for me. All of my strokes are only fair, never great. So it seems to me those good players better start watching themselves and try to only fairly hit the ball. (I must confess that I do on occasion spoon the ball but certainly not on purpose.)

Another rule is that a player cannot accept physical assistance or protection from the elements while trying to whack the ball. (This includes having your partner bend back those branches!)

I imposed this rule when my wife was teeing off right next to some alligators basking in the sun. "Sorry dear, but I can't provide any protection. Rules are rules."

There must exist a fine line between rules and etiquette. For example, it has never been clear to me if it is against the rules to hit your drive when the foursome in front of you is about 150 yards down the fairway or just in bad taste.

71

But if you want to keep your blood pressure down, don't get up on the tee box until it is time to hit. Standing there waiting for the group in front to clear 300 yards is a sure-fire way to hit a 100 yard duck hook. If that's not bad enough, at least two more foursomes will have gathered behind you to watch your long awaited big drive (public courses only).

Another rule/etiquette issue is the gimme. I haven't seen a lot of gimmes in the big tournaments on TV so I suspect it is frowned upon, but nothing could be better for maintaining your composure.

Find a partner who shares your enthusiasm for gimmes, and you will never find yourself sobbing over a missed two foot par putt again.

Of course, we all know that you must putt for a birdie but I rarely encounter a gimme for a birdie anyway. If you do, you might want to stop reading this book now before your entire game is screwed up.

One rule I could never give my full support to is the "out of bounds".

I don't think we should penalize ourselves so severely to protect those rich people's houses on the course. Besides, hitting provisionals just takes up time and no one is going to let you walk back to the tee to hit again if you find your ball across the line. Follow my earlier "modified" rule and just drop, although you might put down two asterisks next to your score.

"...We're here live...to see if he remembers to sign his card."

Speaking of crazy rules, who do you suppose thought up the rule that you have to sign your score card? Even though this doesn't apply to any of you, it is certainly a testament to the inane persistence of the game's rules. 30 million people watching on TV, 200 camera crew from the network TV station filming each shot, gobs of commentators following each player's every move and the poor guy gets disqualified because he doesn't sign the card.

Are they afraid he might be trying to pull a fast one on the world?

Well, the good news is you can ignore this rule also and sign the card only if you feel like it.

A set of rules that I worry about constantly are those rules that govern the loss of my amateur status.

Here again, the rules provide great detail on the ways one can lose your amateur status.

As I was reading the rules, I realized that this book on golf might very well force me into the professional ranks (for accepting money for my writing about how to golf). I no longer will be obligated to refuse to accept prize money or other extravagant gifts or prizes, as I was honored to do as an amateur.

I feel like I've lost a bit of my soul in this transition into the profession.

I just hope Arnie and Jack and Tom and Greg and Tiger and all the others receive me with open arms. I'm one of you, now, guys. (Not bad for someone who can't play the game all that well, eh?)

In summary, most of the rules of golf are meant for people who are serious (obsessed) about the game, and since that is exactly what we are trying to avoid here, I won't continue to lament the irrelevance of the rules to the enjoyment of the game.

***

Chapter 4. Practice

The primary reason for practicing is to hit fewer bad shots that will send your blood pressure through the roof. Your score, as it turns out, will probably never get much better so don't think that is the reason you practice. You might ask, "If I hit fewer bad shots, why doesn't my score go down?" That's a good question. It just doesn't.

But that's no reason not to practice.

Consider, on the other hand, that it can be very calming to know that any bad shot you hit is because you haven't had time to get to the driving range.

T. Joey
PRACTICE MAKES PERFECT!

I would therefore suggest you strategically decide when to practice, such as in the middle of the winter when you're not playing and no one will see you.

But to keep your calm, you must know not only when to practice but also how. For example, be careful about hitting five or seven irons off of a practice mat. You might start to believe that you can actually play the game.

Have you ever noticed how the pro shop salesperson always gives you a five iron to try when they want you to buy those neat new clubs? They even put a little duct tape on the face, hinting at the idea that it is to protect the club face. Poppycock!

That tape makes the ball go nice and straight and they know it. So why not put the tape on your own clubs? Don't even get me started on that rule!!

Nothing creates more frustration than hitting great shots on the practice tee, then shanking shot after shot during your round. Since you probably will never quit making the bad shots during the round, the only other solution is to start hitting worse shots during practice.

One surefire way to do this is to hit lots of long irons and drivers. Don't dwell on that errant good shot, hurry up and hit that next slicing, hooking, dribbling worm killer.

You should also not worry about hitting the short irons. No one except a showoff (good player) practices hitting nine irons or pitching wedges.

Besides, how far can you hit it unless you get a real good blade shot, at which point you should smugly point out to your practice partner that you just hit a nine iron 212 yards and not even the pros do that!

You should also practice off of grass (dirt if you practice where I do) as much as possible. Mats are much too forgiving and will result in too many good shots. This is, of course, not true if you carry a mat with you when you golf and place the ball on it for each shot, but that's usually only practiced in Saudi Arabia and Oklahoma.

The single most common cause for emotional melt-down is the common bunker shot.

And yet, how many of you have seen a public driving range with a sand trap for you to practice in?

The reason is obvious.

These same driving ranges usually sell clubs to replace the ones broken in disgust.

Since I play about one fourth of my shots from the sand during a normal round, I feel that I get sufficient practice on the course.

Sometimes I even stay in the trap for several strokes, the first and second being very short sand shots in a long trap and the final being a blade shot going about 120 yards past the hole.

If you reverse the order of these shots, you won't get nearly as much practice in the sand so stick to the formula.

Practicing your putting makes great sense as half of all shots are putts.

On the other hand, you're never going to get it so why bother. And it isn't even your fault.

When the grand marshals of golf were dreaming up all those silly rules that penalize you for every little thing, why didn't they make rules for the golf courses that said all greens had to be the same?

How do they expect you to putt when they put bumps and dips all over the green, and they all go at different speeds! So no matter how much you practice, the next green is going to be totally different!

In my case, the courses I play also have aeration holes just slightly smaller than the cup which result in some curious breaks. Practicing bumper pool isn't a bad way to prepare for these courses.

READING A FRESHLY AERATED GREEN

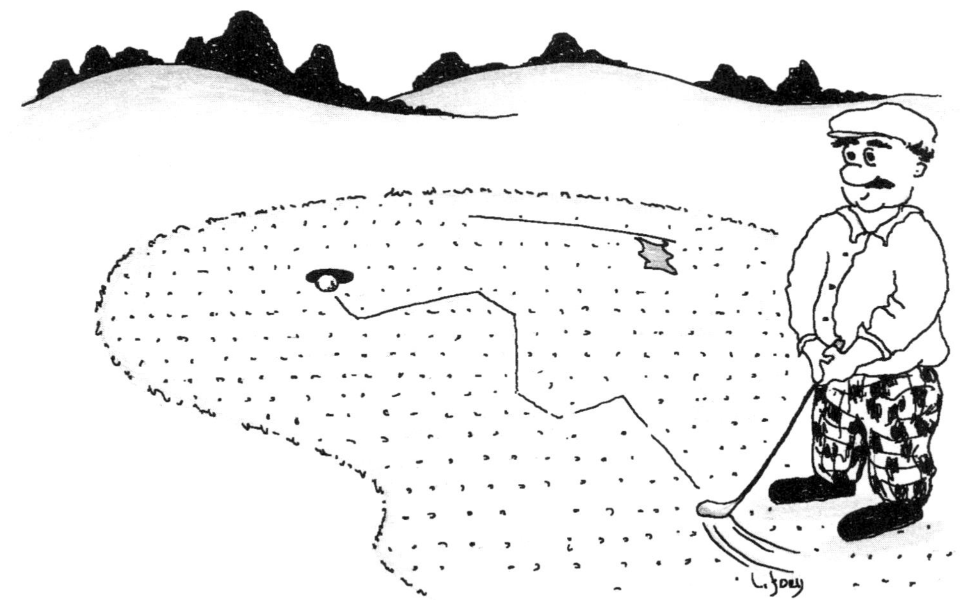

-In summary-

Practice ugly and play better and you'll keep a cool head.

***

Chapter 5. Opponents/Partners

This section does not apply to tournaments since you have little to say about whom you play against in a tournament and tournaments are discussed in Chapter 7.

What we are talking about here are the people you routinely play with for fun. One obvious choice is your spouse. I could take the easy way out and say that playing with your spouse is a disaster waiting to happen.

On the contrary, if you follow the suggestions in this book, you'll find that golfing with your spouse is a pleasant experience.

If you don't, the National Enquirer actually might be too embarrassed to run the story of your breakup.

Spousal golf, however, does require one or two special tips to keep everyone calm. For example, you must be careful not to suggest improvements to your spouse's swing. Once you do, you are on the hook for every bad shot in the future.

I made this mistake once, suggesting a fuller back-swing to get more power into her stroke. It wasn't until the next day that the problems started. After many holes of bad swings and growling snarls, I begged her to take a shorter swing. I confessed to making a terrible mistake and hinted at the influence of the Devil that made me tell her such a stupid thing.

Just keep quiet.
Stay calm.
No need to panic.

"What do you think I'm
doing wrong sweety?"

L. Joey

Although I was ultimately forgiven (six months and twelve days later) it was an awful experience!

TIP

When asked for help by your wife, feign a heat stroke or in cool weather start rummaging through your bag looking for a sweater. Be sure not to make eye contact or exhibit any signs of fear. They can smell panic.

But not all of your partners will be your spouse!

(I'm still talking about golf here)

As suggested earlier, there are some characteristics of a partner that are desirable and some that aren't.

Look for someone who understands the importance of the gimme and the Mulligan.

These very important gestures are most effective if they come from your partner rather than you. Nothing sounds nicer than a cheerful "that's a gimme" or "I think there was a fly on the ball, why don't you take a Mulligan".

Of course your partner expects the same in return, so be generous.

THE IDEAL PLAYING PARTNER
"Sorry, I was breathing hard.
Why don't you take a Mulligan."

Another important trait of a good playing partner is one who plays at a similar pace to your own.

If you're one of those people who takes fifteen practice swings, steps up to the ball then backs off because a wisp of wind came up, wiggles your butt, waggles your club, then asks one more time for the exact yardage and changes clubs - all the while the people behind you are dropping from heat stroke waiting to hit - then find someone who does the same.

You deserve each other and neither of you will lose your composure. However, if you play up smartly, be sure to avoid the slow type like the plague.

If you don't, you'll find your teeth gnashing and eyes sadly glancing back to the foursome behind you, wishing you could let them know it isn't you going through these routines that could only be choreographed off-off-Broadway.

When I taught my wife to play (not a good idea), the first lesson was how to play fast. We are now totally compatible in pace, except when I'm off in the bushes looking for my ball and she's hitting those very unimaginative shots up the middle of the fairway.

The other important factor in choosing a good playing partner is the person's skill level.

Be sure to try to find people a lot better than you once in a while and treat it as a practice lesson.

You might also play with far inferior golfers on occasion, and this would be the only time you break my rule about keeping score.

But for the most part you should stick with someone of comparable ability. This way you can compete comfortably (match play, never total score) and not have to worry about handicapping.

Even though you're comparable, this should not deter you from getting as many strokes as possible in your match.

DECIDING WHEN TO KEEP SCORE

"Wanna keep score today?"

Of course the best way to play the game is to never keep score and announce at the end of the round that you think you were a couple of strokes better. If you try this too often, however, you might need to find a new partner. Another important trait to look for in a partner is good eyesight. This can save you dozens of balls in the course of a year.

Of course the other extreme is also workable.

If your partner has terrible eyesight just direct him to the poorer of the two shots and he'll never know the difference. Be sure you are the one to pick up the balls at the end of the hole so you can give him his ball back.

Probably the most important trait of a playing partner is that they like to treat you to hot dogs and drinks before, during and after the game.

As you can see, picking your playing partner should not be taken lightly. Proper selection can result in more wins, more food, lower scores and a good time.

Unfortunately, as more people read this book they will also be looking for ideal partners and you will probably get a lot more of "No thanks, I'm going to the Flower Show with my wife and her friends."

***

Chapter 6. Courses

I have not played a lot of courses so this chapter will be rather brief. However, look for my sequel "The Top Courses in the U.S." That would pay my way to play them. It should be coming out as soon as the course managers start sending me offers to play their beautiful courses just for a favorable mention. (I might need several rounds at Pebble to get the real feel of the course.)

In recent years I have played courses primarily in three locations. The first is local to where I live. I can only get onto public courses and mostly on the weekend, so we're talking about a five to six hour ordeal.

These are necessary evils to keep your game finely honed in the low 90's (if you're still in the 100's you need to read the part on free drops more carefully).

To enjoy golf at these courses requires lots of patience, stamina and preferably a frontal lobotomy.

To make these courses more tolerable, try taking distractions. A cellular phone can allow you to get a lot of those pesky business calls out of the way, especially if it is a work day afternoon and your boss thinks you're at a client's office. However, make sparing use of the cell phone on the greens and tee boxes while people are hitting. For some reason, talking has still not become acceptable background noise in golf.

MIXING BUSINESS WITH PLEASURE
"Go ahead, patch me into the conference call."
L. Joay

The laptop computer offers a myriad of opportunities for keeping busy while in the middle of a slow round. For example, I wrote most of this book on the 8th and 9th holes of a particularly slow round.

Be sure to turn off all those cute little noises that Windows® has going off without warning. They can be somewhat distracting to your partner.

But the reality is that you can only compensate so much for the tedium of playing local public courses (For those of you who live in places like Myrtle Beach, Hilton Head, Jacksonville, Tucson, or Phoenix, you are the exception to the rule.) It will sooner or later start to wear on your patience and then your emotional stability will start to unravel.

The other two places I play golf consistently but not often are Hilton Head and the Bahamas. Quite by accident we have discovered unique times when golfing at these places for the sake of enjoyment is at its best. We go to Hilton Head during the week of Christmas. The weather is usually fine to great and the courses are relatively uncrowded. This is a great chance to play a number of excellent courses at reduced rates. We routinely play a round in 3 to 4 hours, even if we are paired up with someone else.

The best part is that it really is winter so the gloves come off with respect to winter rules. If you are one of those people or couples who plays slowly, don't go to Hilton Head during this time. You might end up in front of me!

For relaxing golf, however, nothing beats our annual trek to Treasure Cay on Abaco Island in the Bahamas. We go at the end of June and almost no one is on the course with us. On our last trip we finished 27 holes in less than 4 hours. And that was with a few trips into the jungle for lost balls (mine obviously). The course is acceptable, the people are great and the sun is hot.

If you want to try new shots, teach your kids to play or just cruise around and enjoy the game, this place can't be beat. I'm quite sure there are many off-season places like this waiting to be discovered.

(Maybe that should be the next book!)

On occasion I get the opportunity to play a desert course. (The first time I played one of these I misunderstood and thought I was going to get an ice cream sundae or something.) These courses are usually target golf, which means you have a little patch of grass out there about 220 yards and you're supposed to hit it with your drive.

Once you navigate your way to the "landing area", you then get to hit your next shot at a postage stamp of grass with a green on it. The good news about these courses is that you can miss the fairway by 20 yards and with the right bounce off a rock you can end up back in the fairway. Be careful about hitting your ball if it appears to be slithering away.

I discourage you from playing the majestic courses on the ocean, such as in California, Bermuda, or maybe Hawaii until you have fully mastered my techniques for maintaining your composure. Acts of incoherent outrage can result in the loss of equipment and possibly even a golfer from time to time.

But once you are a master of calmness, you should definitely play these courses. The scenery is spectacular enough to let you forget your playing skills for months to come.

You can also show your friends pictures of these courses when you get back and make their lives just a little more miserable, which of course is always good for your own state of mind.

108

BE SURE YOU NEVER KEEP SCORE ON TROPICAL COURSES.

If you happen to shoot well (not likely), you can always make up a score at the end.

***

Chapter 7. Handicaps

The title of this chapter probably means different things to different people. Some of you immediately thought of your spouse. Others had visions of their severe hook on any hole that has out-of-bounds to the left. Although these are, without question, major handicaps to some of you, it doesn't have anything to do with this chapter.

What I am, in fact, referring to is an elaborate means used by golf clubs (not the clubs you use but the groups you belong to) to grade people on their golf game. It is meant to make all of us equal in the eyes of the "Net score" with some edge to the better golfer.

HANDICAPPING AT ITS BEST

This is an intriguing concept except I don't understand who cares. If you let me fight the best boxers in the world and I get to be armed with meat cleavers in each hand, I'd probably win about half the time. Does that prove anything except that even with a huge advantage I still can't win consistently?

The real question is who thought up the concept of handicapping. Was it the good guys because they got tired of playing with the few other good players? Or was it a lousy player who was looking for that rush resulting from sinking that last putt for a 98 to crush the guy who shot a 74? Both of these groups of golfers have good reasons, but there was probably another group involved in the evolution of handicapping.

Think for a moment about all those tournament directors out there trying to put together enough entrants for the "Good Player Tournament". Or the embarrassment of having to sign up on the list for the next tournament scheduled -- "The Crummy Players Tournament".

Other sports, such as tennis or racquetball, suffer from the same problems and have resorted to letter labeling ("I'm in the A draw. Are you still playing Ds?") or numbering schemes ("I'm a 4.379 player. Anyone here 4.3 to 4.4?").

Bowling, however, is structured similarly to golf except for the requirement to drink beer during the tournament.

ORGANIZING TOURNAMENTS WITHOUT HANDICAPS

The good thing about golf handicapping is that it is totally irrelevant if you are not interested in playing in tournaments, although I have heard a lot of men talking about their handicaps who could not have possibly been interested in playing seriously. For those of you who insist on playing in tournaments despite my strong recommendations against it, here are a few words of advice about establishing a handicap.

First, no matter how much people like to brag about a low handicap, the fact is that bigger is better.

If you really want to win a tournament, it isn't going to be with a handicap established with the ten best rounds of your life.

So this is where you take all of my rules for playing with self generosity and reverse them. You should relish the bad lie, not fix it. If your ball is on that out of bounds line, nail yourself. And whatever you do, never take gimmes. Putting every putt should add at least one or two strokes to your handicap.

Now some might say "Wait! Hold it one minute. I thought these things would drive you crazy and you would have a heart attack." That's true. That's what will happen to you when you actually play the tournament and you start shanking those same shots. But during handicap rounds, your mind set must be totally altered to view these problems as pluses rather than minuses.

ESTABLISHING A HANDICAP

Don't misunderstand me. I'm not suggesting that you sandbag, i.e., play intentionally poorly or report only bad rounds. I have enough confidence in you to know that you can generate lots of bad scores without these immoral acts. Just go about your business and let nature take its course.

If you don't belong to a club that establishes handicaps or you simply don't want to take the time to do so, there are still ways to take part in the repartee in the clubhouse.

If you are trying to impress someone (but be sure to never play a match with these people) just say you think your handicap would be about 11.

If you said 6, they might want to play with you to pick up some pointers. If you said 18, no one is going to be impressed. So 11 is a good compromise. As it turns out, no one in the world has a handicap of 11. If you're good, you are below ten. If you aren't, you're above 15. People only hit 11 on their way up or down! If you are trying to hustle someone for a few strokes at the start of a match, just claim 18-20 as needed depending on your opponent's claim. These are good numbers because they are low enough to let you hit just about any score and claim it was a fluke but not too high to get you punched in the nose.

These tips might sound sneaky but the unfortunate fact is that without a mainframe computer you probably don't have a clue as to your real handicap.

"It's calculated how?"

If ever questioned about your claim, just indicate that it probably has to do with the slope of the course (difficulty, not tilt) and that should end the conversation.

If your opponent continues to press, point out that you prefer to play match play anyway so the handicap becomes less important.

Suggest that you just take a stroke a hole and let bygones be bygones.

***

Chapter 8. Tournaments

This is a tough chapter to write since it goes against everything I have preached, but it is a subject that must be dealt with. Actually, if your urges for tournament play are properly channeled, you can still maintain a calm and relaxed approach to the game.

The strongest recommendation I can make is to seek out tournaments based on the scramble format.

Some of you might know these tournaments by different names, but the general format is that teams of four play together and shoot each shot from the position of the best shot of all four's prior shots.

Assembling the Scramble Team

This basically translates to - you can make as many bad shots as you want and still have a good score as a team.

Of course, as in any team sport, the secret to success is in the selection of your team members.

Another neat thing about these tournaments is that they usually have lots of prizes, even for the losers.

Seek these tournaments out with a vengeance.

If you still have an itching for tournament play, then first get in a few tournaments that aren't handicapped and you don't have a prayer of winning.

This conditions you to the feeling of not doing well, a feeling that you will come to know many times in the future.

Once that feeling of defacto losing has been established, you can then start thinking about establishing your handicap (see preceding chapter) and playing in the club handicapped tournaments.

You still won't have a prayer in the world, but now you're conditioned for really losing big time.

As you play in more tournaments it will become increasingly important to have ways to check your level of absorption.

... so then I pull out my 3 iron on the
13th fairway, thinking if I could just...

If you find your spouse dozing off face first into the mashed potatoes while you provide a stroke by stroke description of your round, you're getting into trouble.

If you are spending more time practicing your putting in your office than doing your work, you're in big trouble. But if you suddenly realize in the middle of an important business meeting that you have been talking about golf while they have been talking about a major business deal, you better cancel out of tournaments and reread this book from cover to cover (preferably buy another copy).

***

Chapter 9. Wagering

Interestingly enough, the rules of golf do not forbid wagering. In fact, they make a distinction between playing for a pool of money in an amateur tournament and placing wagers on yourself or your team.

The first will get you in big trouble and you'll have to give up all those tournaments for amateurs (see the chapter on NOT playing in tournaments).

The second form of wagering is okay with the rules as long as only the players lay out the dough and you're only playing for fun (wink, wink). Unfortunately, my loyal following can no longer kick in a few bucks.

(I assume they were betting on me!)

Note that the policy does not mention the legality of gambling, which apparently is up to the states to enforce. Even though most states do not permit gambling, this is not usually a problem since the state's resources are tied up in administering their lotteries.

But there have been many recent instances related to high profile people betting very large sums of money on golf. It appears to me that even the rules people suggest that betting is part of the game. However, we are talking here about keeping the blood pressure in check, so if you don't have a hundred grand to spare, don't get involved in the big time betting.

Here is an effective way to play for money with a diverse group of players (that means some are crappy and some are not quite so crappy). It's called Bingo, Bango, Bongo. Each hole has three possible points and hitting by honors must be strictly enforced (I don't know what the consequences would be if you didn't, but it sounded very official).

The first point (Bingo) is awarded to the person who is first on the green. People with good approach shots (I'm not talking about your fifth shot to the green) have a distinct advantage here.

The second point (Bango) is awarded to the person closest to the pin after everyone is on the green.

Those of you who don't quite seem to get on the green with your approach shot but you can chip well are looking good on this one.

The final point (Bongo) goes to the person who is first in the hole. This one is interesting. If you're good at lagging those long putts right up next to the hole, you're out of luck (I consider this poetic justice).

In preparation for these types of matches I have perfected putting where I'm no closer than six feet to the pin after my first putt. This usually gives me the first serious shot at sinking the Bongo putt. Sometimes I even get two chances in a row!

I told you putting wasn't my strength.

If wagering,
choose your opponent carefully

The end result of all these points should be a fairly even match without the agony of establishing handicaps (see earlier chapter).

One way to look at wagering is that it is a modest addition to the exorbitant cost of playing a decent round of golf nowadays. If you play on an overcast, threatening day, you're already wagering a substantial amount on the weather holding up. If you're playing a nice course with one of those snack women going around in a cart (for those of you who have not yet experienced this, it is the ultimate luxury), keep the winnings in a pool and use it to tip the lady. It makes her happy and takes the pressure off of you about what to do with all that money you win.

***

Chapter 10. Golf and Politicians

Note: This chapter is not the same as the next chapter so please read both carefully, especially if you are the President or anticipate becoming the President.

Consider the fact that our forefathers cleverly structured the government so that about half of the Congress is obligated to find every way possible to sabotage the President and the other half wants his job as head of the party when he gets the boot.

In recent history, presidents have come under fire for a number of immoral and/or illegal acts. These attacks are championed by other politicians or media people whose sole purpose is to protect the public and maintain the high standards of morality observed by others in the political and media professions. (Personal fame or fortune never plays a role.)

In many of these attacks, the issue at hand has had to do with the sexual exploits of the President. This trend will certainly continue as the Baby Boomers enjoy more and more political power.

One can assume that the Baby Boomers will continue to rule the roost for many years to come. But as they become older, the idea that they have sexual exploits becomes far less plausible. That's where I think golf will come in.

BIG NEWS
PRESIDENT
ALTERS SCORE
CARD!!

Our Presidents will want, perhaps even need, to play golf and golf is a game of high moral standards. (except when I'm playing)

So one might expect that the press and the opposing party will fall back on golf to try to establish immorality and distrust. (Please notice incompetence is rarely the issue, given the fact that it is almost impossible to determine if a politician is in fact doing anything constructive)

Could we, a country of high moral character, be expected to tolerate a President in office that cheats on the golf course or reports an incorrect score?

I think not!

Sure, we can overlook a few brushes with the IRS or indictments by a variety of special prosecutors, but let's watch that scorekeeping.

I therefore recommend that if you are a high level politician, you accurately keep score. This might even mean keeping track of all those pesky little penalty strokes and not placing the ball where it is much more convenient to hit.

And don't have your aides do the dirty work for you. They'll spill their guts on the stand when the prosecutor starts grilling them on your last round at the club. I also would like to suggest you keep those scary guys with the sunglasses and suits far away from the course when you go golfing.

Such a display of social **import** (you should learn to use this word whenever possible; it shows high intellect and total disregard for readability, making it particularly well suited for this chapter) will undoubtedly make it harder for you to hustle a few extra strokes out of your opponent. To get more strokes, lament about how late you were up planning bombing raids and you think it is starting to affect your concentration. If that doesn't work, threaten your opponent to a life of misery in a weather station outside of Nome, Alaska. After all, you are the President. It has to have some perks.

One of the advantages you have as a high level politician is that your tension level is already at extraordinary levels and playing golf could only bring it down.

But enough about politicians.

After all, they are people just like you or me.

Their government limousine is no different from the rest of our limos, and our body guards would take a bullet for us just like their's would.

And I'm sure that it costs about 2 million dollars every time you want to go to Barbados or Hawaii for a nice round of relaxing golf.

So don't envy or pity this small band of misfit mega-lomaniacs, but rather sharpen up that commanding voice of yours in the event you play with Mr. President and you need to snappily yell:

That's a gimme, sir!!

***

Chapter 11. Golf and Sex

My publisher explained to me that any book will sell better with a little sex in it, so I've devoted this entire chapter to it. Here's my first observation:

Golf and Sex are both good, but not usually together!

My publisher also strongly suggested using a double entendre in the book. Since I had to look up double entendre, which took quite a long while thanks to a really stupid spelling, I don't think I'll try one of those in this book.

I've asked a consultant to research some clever ones so I should have something ready in about six months. (Boy, $50,000 doesn't go as far as it used to).

As with any sport, profession, activity ... (you get the picture, just about anything) . . . men <u>will</u> fantasize about women!

<u>Golf is no different</u>. Despite the fact that a reasonably intelligent man (of which there are several) must realize that nothing is going to happen out there on the course, he will still dream of that fantasy day when playing alone and he is asked to join three gorgeous nymphomaniacs from Wisconsin.

Since this fantasizing seems to be an inevitable burden born by men (a little sympathy from the women here wouldn't hurt), they must learn to control or redirect these urges.

I believe the naked lady tees can be of some assistance, but if that fails, carry large bags of ice to be strategically positioned. This might also help you keep your head down and arm stiff.

A GOLF FANTASY

SEX and MOVING CARTS...

...the inevitable consequence.

Now, this was going to be the end of this chapter, since I have very strong religious convictions about mentioning sex in mixed company, but after reading the sex material my publisher said, "This is great stuff. Do you have any more insights?"

So I sat down and devoted another 2 months to what I think might just turn your life around. (This is just a teaser to keep you reading. Actually nothing will ever improve your sex life. Hence the importance of playing golf.)

It turns out that what has always appeared obvious to me about golf and sex is not so obvious to others. For example, I instinctively knew a moving golf cart and having sex was bound to result in a very bad accident and possibly even embarrassment or bodily injury to someone. Therefore I suggest you avoid this situation.

I believe the government recently launched a national program for safe sex which is apparently directed at this very issue. With every problem comes an opportunity.

If you have a big match to play, be sure to enlist the services of the most voluptuous woman golfer you know. Ask her to join you in your outing and make sure your opponent rides with her in the cart.

Even though he might enjoy his game more than you do, you just might pull out a win.

"You'll be riding with Bambi... we'll be playing for $4.00 a hole."
L. Joey

Of course if she beats both of you soundly you might feel a bit more tension, so be sure to check her golfing credentials carefully before asking her to join you.

There isn't a whole lot else to say about sex (either related to golf or not).

If you're reading this book with the hopes of getting guidance for your sex life, you've got problems way way beyond the scope of this book anyway.

***

12. Epilog

It's always important to end a book with lots and lots of surprising and perhaps heart rending material.

In our particular case, the twist to the plot is that even after reading this profound and inspiring work, you will still go out and flail and wail, lose all of your composure and threaten to give up the stupid game of golf . . . forever.

Take, for example, the typical round of Joe Golfer.

His scorecard has more snowmen on it than a park in New York City after a big snow.

Then he comes to the 18th tee.

He's frustrated, exhausted, sunburned, windburned, his feet are soaked from wading in the lakes, he has pine needles in his hair and he just wants to get home so he can burn the clubs.

(note: modern clubs don't burn that well)

He addresses the ball, not nearly as respectfully as he has in the past.

He draws the club back, letting his left arm bend ON PURPOSE, and lets rip as hard as he can, exactly what all those pros have told him not to do!

THE FINAL DRIVE

But wait! What's this? The ball clinks crisply off the face of his club. His hands don't even feel the impact. The ball starts off not up or down, left or right, but out and up, climbing at a steady rate with only a slight draw, giving the ball a little extra roll. It seems to sail forever, then drops back to earth, landing gently and rolling another 40 yards down the middle of the fairway. He gasps for air. His head swoons. His buddies all murmur a "WOW" and he feels a rush like no other he's ever felt. (sorry Mrs. Golfer, but it's true)

This is what it's all about! He's discovered the secret!

THE SECRET ?

What did he do?

He thinks he swung a little inside out, or maybe he teed it higher this time. No, no, he played it more off his left toe. Or was it in the middle of his stance? He's sure it was that bent left arm!

He'll get a par on that final hole, and all the way home he'll be thinking about that next fantastic round, when it finally all comes together and he breaks 90!

The End

> **"Golf is a game that creates emotions that sometimes cannot be sustained with the club still in one's hand."**
>
> -Bobby Jones

Note:

I want all of you Hollywood executives to know that I have reserved the movie rights to this book so please contact me directly about any offers.

Special Note:

I would prefer if Tom Selleck played me but I'm always open to suggestions.

Extra Special Note:

Tom Cruise might also work.

***

Happy Golfing

About the Author

Bill Kennish has a Doctorate in Engineering, has never broken 80 in golf (except on an easy miniature golf course), has absolutely no background in psychology and has never written a book before. We hope you read this page before buying the whole story!

His almost, but not quite, award winning doctoral thesis dealt with the use of quasilinearization techniques for parameter identification in modeling nonlinear viscoelastic materials. First edition copies are still available upon request. (He made two copies).

About the Illustrator

Lisa Joey's passion for art has taken her through an adventurous life of challenges and media, from crayons to designing porcelain and gold crowns. The opportunity to illustrate this book fulfills a childhood dream, besides allowing her to learn a new game. She has never hit a ball, let alone swung a club, but she has done several rounds on the links with a Frisbee.

OTHER FUN BOOKS

A whimsical collection of delightful books to
make you think, chuckle, self-motivate & lift your spirits.

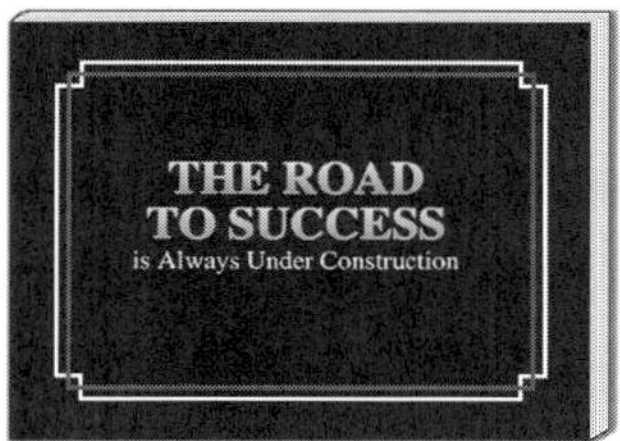

The Road to Success

Motherhood

Achieve Your Dreams

Computer Byte?

View from Litter Box

Doggie Tales

ORDER ADDITIONAL BOOKS AS GIFTS

GOLFING
for the Emotionally Impaired   Qty_______ @ 7.95 Each _________

COMPUTER BYTE   Qty_______ @ 7.95 Each _________

THE ROAD TO SUCCESS   Qty_______ @ 7.95 Each _________

ACHIEVE YOUR DREAMS   Qty_______ @ 7.95 Each _________

MOTHERHOOD   Qty_______ @ 7.95 Each _________

VIEW FROM LITTER BOX   Qty_______ @ 7.95 Each _________

KITTY LITTERATURE   Qty_______ @ 7.95 Each _________

DOGGIE TALES   Qty_______ @ 7.95 Each _________

MONEY   Qty_______ @ 7.95 Each _________

GARDEN GROW   Qty_______ @ 7.95 Each _________

Add 2.00 for shipping for 1st book, 50¢ ea. thereafter _________

WA State residents only: add applicable sales tax
Canadian & Foreign orders: double S & H charges & pay in US Funds
Order by phone: MasterCard / VISA accepted

www.walrusproductions.com   Total__________

Walrus Productions
4805 N.E. 106th St
Seattle, WA 98125
(206) 364-4365

Name ___________________________

Address ___________________________

City ___________________________

State / Zip ___________________________

Prices subject to change

These books may be ordered through your local book store.